W9-BIU-793

PLANTERS

By E. T. Weingarten

Gareth Stevens
PUBLISHING

Please visit our website, www.garethstevens.com. For a free color catalog of all our high-quality books, call toll free 1-800-542-2595 or fax 1-877-542-2596.

Library of Congress Cataloging-in-Publication Data

Names: Weingarten, E. T., author.
Title: Planters / E.T. Weingarten.
Other titles: Fantastic farm machines.
Description: New York : Gareth Stevens Publishing, [2016] | Series: Fantastic
  farm machines | Includes index.
Identifiers: LCCN 2016003829 | ISBN 9781482445947 (pbk.) | ISBN 9781482445855
(library bound) | ISBN 9781482445732 (6 pack)
Subjects: LCSH: Planters (Agricultural machinery)–Juvenile literature.
Classification: LCC TJ1483 .W45 2016 | DDC 681/.7631–dc23
LC record available at http://lccn.loc.gov/2016003829

Published in 2017 by
Gareth Stevens Publishing
111 East 14th Street, Suite 349
New York, NY 10003

Designer: Sarah Liddell
Editor: Therese Shea

Photo credits: Cover, p. 1 Zorandim/Shutterstock.com; spread background texture used throughout LongQuattro/Shutterstock.com; p. 5 Singkham/Shutterstock.com; pp. 7, 13 smereka/Shutterstock.com; p. 9 Scott Olson/Staff/Getty Images News/ Getty Images; p. 11 afnr/Shutterstock.com; p. 15 Feddacheenee/Wikimedia Commons; p. 17 B Brown/Shutterstock.com; p. 19 Nancy Nehring/Contributor/ Moment Mobile/Getty Images; p. 21 (air seeder) Jeff Zenner Photography/ Shutterstock.com; p. 21 (seed drill) Baloncici/Shutterstock.com.

Printed in the United States of America

CPSIA compliance information: Batch #CS16GS: For further information contact Gareth Stevens, New York, New York at 1-800-542-2595.

CONTENTS

Boldface words appear in the glossary.

Plenty of Planting

Have you ever planted a garden? You likely dug holes, placed seeds in them, and covered them with dirt. Can you picture doing that again and again on a farm? Rather than digging holes themselves, farmers use **fantastic** machines.

Helpful Machines

Planters are farm machines that sow, or plant, seeds to grow crops. A planter is towed through a field by a tractor. Planters can be small or large. They can plant one row of seeds or many rows.

Planter Parts

All planters, small and large, share certain features. They have one or more seed boxes that hold the seeds that will be sown. The planter may have a seed box for each row or one seed box that supplies seeds for all rows.

seed boxes

There are special wheels in each row of a planter. The trash wheel cleans out anything in the dirt in the row. Next, blades called the disc opener dig a **trench**. Then, the **gauge** wheel makes the seed drop into the right place.

11

Finally, the closing wheels push dirt over the seeds. Planters can allow different spaces between seeds if needed. They may be set to place more or less space between rows, too. Different crops may need different amounts of space.

seed box

gauge wheel

trash wheel

disc opener

closing wheel

Amazing Planters

Some planters are really wide. The largest in the world is about 120 feet (37 m) wide. It can sow 48 rows at once! This planter can plant a field quickly, but it costs a lot of money. It's worth more than $300,000!

24-row planter

There are planters with **sensors** that tell farmers the number of seeds they've planted. There are planters that carry and drop **fertilizer** for the crops, too. Some planters can even sow two kinds of crops at once.

potato planter

17

There are planters controlled by computers that tell exactly where to plant in a field. This is helpful for farmers with trees and other objects in their fields. Computers can also help planters make corn **mazes** like the one shown here!

More Ways to Sow

Planters aren't the only planting machines. Air seeders use air to blow seeds into the soil. Seed drills use blades to drill into the soil before sowing seeds. We're lucky that farmers have such fantastic farm machines!

air seeder

seed drill

21

GLOSSARY

fantastic: great, wonderful

fertilizer: something that makes soil better for growing crops and other plants

gauge: a tool for measuring an amount

maze: an area of connected paths that is hard to find a way through

sensor: a tool that can sense changes in its surroundings

trench: a long, deep hole dug into the ground

FOR MORE INFORMATION

BOOKS

Borth, Teddy. *Machines on the Farm*. Minneapolis, MN: ADBO, 2015.

Dayton, Connor. *Planters*. New York, NY: PowerKids Press, 2012.

Kuskowski, Alex. *Super Simple Kitchen Gardens: A Kid's Guide to Gardening*. Minneapolis, MN: ABDO Publishing, 2015.

WEBSITES

How Does a Planter Work?
blog.mlive.com/freshfood/2012/05/how_does_a_planter_work.html
Read more about the parts of a planter.

Types of Seeders
farmingequipmentcanada.com/farming-equipment-canada/types-of-seeders/
Read about other tools farmers use to sow seeds.

INDEX